NOEL MACHIN

African Poetry
for Schools

BOOK ONE

LONGMAN

Longman Group UK Limited,
Longman House, Burnt Mill, Harlow,
Essex CM20 2JE, England
and Associated Companies throughout the world.

© Longman Group Limited 1978
All rights reserved; no part of this publication
may be reproduced, stored in a retrieval system,
or transmitted in any form or by any means, electronic,
mechanical, photocopying, recording, or otherwise,
without the prior written permission of the Publishers.

First published 1978
Tenth impression 1987

Set in 11/13 pt Apollo (Monophoto)

Produced by Longman Group (FE) Limited
Printed in Hong Kong

ISBN 0-582-60163-0

Contents

Acknowledgements

We are grateful to the following for permission to reproduce copyright material:

Beacon Press for an extract from an anonymous poem in *Umbundu: Folk Tales From Angola* by Merlin Ennis. Copyright © 1962 by Merlin Ennis. Reprinted by permission of Beacon Press; Cambridge University Press for five riddles from *Yoruba Poetry* by U. Beier 1970; The author for his poem 'Streamside Exchange' by Dr. John Pepper Clark; The author for an extract from his poem 'Spider' by Frank Collymore in *Caribbean Voices* edited by J. Figuerson 1966 Vol. 1; East African Publishing House for an extract from an untitled poem by Agostinho Neto in *When Bullets Begin to Flower* by Margaret Dickinson and for the poem 'Beggar' by A. Kassam in *Drumbeat* edited by Lennard Okala; Heinemann Educational Books Ltd. for an adapted extract from *Myths And Legends Of The Congo* by J. Knappert, for an extract from a poem in *The Wound* by M. Fall, two anonymous poems from *Igbo Traditional Verse* by R. Egudo & D. Nwoga, an extract from the poem 'The Beloved' by A. R. Cliff-Lubwa P'Chong from *Poems From East Africa* edited by Cook & Rubadiri, an extract from an untitled poem by I. Choonara from *Seven South African Poets* edited by C. Pieterse and for an extract from the chainsong in *Arrow Of God* by Chinua Achebe; Author's Agent for the poem 'Give Me A Chair . . .' anonymous from *An African Treasury* edited by Langston Hughes; Ghana Publishing Corporation for two poems entitled 'The Stem Of The Branch' and *'Yaa, The Adowa Dancer* by L. M. Asiedu in *Talent For Tomorrow* 1970; Ibadan University Press for an anonymous poem in *Yoruba Poetry* edited by Gbadomosi & Beier and for a poem by Pious Oleghe in *Nigerian Student Verse* edited by M. Banham 1959; Indiana University Press Book Publishers for an extract from the poem 'Palm Leaves Of Childhood' by G. Adali-Mortti from *Poems From Black Africa* edited by Langston Hughes © 1963 by Langston Hughes. Reprinted by permission of Indiana University Press, Bloomington; Longman Group Ltd. for an extract from *The Dilemma Of A Ghost* by C. A. Aidoo; David McKay Company Inc. for three poems from *Echoes Of Africa* by B. Landeck 1969. Reprinted by permission of the publisher; Oxford University Press for a poem entitled 'I am An Honest African' by Shabban Robert in *Swahili Poetry* 1962 by Lyndon Harries and for twelve untitled poems from *Oral Literature In Africa* by Ruth Finnegan; Random House Inc. for the poem 'Madam and Her Madam' from *Selected Poems* by Langston Hughes; The Author for the poem 'Love Song' by Henri-Philippe Junod translated by Willard R. Trask and the translator for the poems 'Lullaby', 'Drum Song' and 'Song Of The Animal World' all anonymous, translated by Willard R. Trask from *The Unwritten*

Song Vol. 1. 1969; Walker and Company Inc. for an extract from *Ants Will Not Eat Your Fingers* by L. W. Doob © 1966 by L. W. Doob and Weidenfeld (Publishers) Ltd. for an extract from a poem in *Primitive Songs* translated by C. M. Bowra. Published by George Weidenfeld and Nicolson Ltd.

We regret that we have been unable to trace the copyright holders of the poem 'Spider' by Jean-Joseph Rabearivelo in *A Book of African Verse* edited by Reed and Wake and would appreciate any information that would enable us to do so.

The Publishers are also grateful to the following for permission to reproduce copyright photographs:

Barnaby's Picture Library for pages 29/30, 47; Camera Press Ltd. for pages 1 (Beni Trutmann), 3/4 (Beni Trutmann), 12 (Raoul Duval), 16 (Peter Mitchell), 20 (John Goldblatt), 62 (Jan Kopec); J. Allan Cash for pages 25/26, 42, 64; G. Chapman for page 56; Bruce Coleman for pages 21 left (Jane Burton), 21 right (G. D. Plage), 28 (Simon Trevor), 52 (Jeff Foott); William Collins and Sons Ltd. for page 13 (W. H. Stevens); Mary Evans Picture Library for page 8; Werner Forman Archive for page 36; Ghana Information Services for page 39; John Hillelson Agency Ltd. for page 44; Alan Hutchison Library for page 50; The Mansell Collection for page 58; Rex Features Ltd. for page 23; Dr. B. Sparkes for pages 17/18. Cover photo: Hoa-Qui Agence, Paris.

We regret that we have been unable to trace the copyright holder of the photograph on page 65 and apologise for any infringement of copyright caused.

Introduction

This is the first of a two-volume anthology of African poetry, in which I have interpreted the word 'African' very broadly, to include the Afro-American world as well as Africa itself.

The poems are arranged in rising order of difficulty in language and subject-matter. The Pupils' and Teacher's Notes have been written with this in mind, so that classes are gradually introduced to simple and then more complex aspects of poetry. Notes for the pupil follow on immediately from each poem and the Teacher's Notes are listed at the end of the book.

1   Most of these poems are written to be *read aloud*. This is most important, because poetry has to do with sound as well as sense, and very often the sound leads us to the sense. Much of the time in class should be spent helping pupils to read aloud in an intelligent, lively way. Many of the poems are dramatic; some are like miniature plays and should be *acted*. This is not an 'extra': it is an essential step towards fulfilling the poem's function.

2   In order to read a poem aloud properly, it must be *understood*. I suggest that the teacher uses the following method: (i) read the poem through once (aloud) either with the class as a whole, or by calling upon individual pupils; (ii) go through it with them slowly, helping them to explain its sense (except with nonsense poems!) and discussing difficult points; (iii) prepare for a proper reading (aloud) by discussing with them whether it should be quiet or lively, frightening or soothing, serious or comic, etc., and deciding which parts need a special emphasis or different treatment; (iv) have a performance—more than one, in the case of a short poem.

3   If pupils understand the poem well enough to give a good performance of it, the teacher's work is virtually done (teaching poetry is not too hard!). Some poems require a whole class-period before this point is reached, while others will take considerably less. In the latter case, the class can discuss matters arising from the poem: whether they agree with what is said in it, whether they think it is said well, and what their own ideas are on the subject. Suggestions for discussion are given in both sets of Notes.

4   While they are learning to understand and enjoy poetry, pupils should also be learning to *write* it. By poetry here, I mean no more than a vivid and expressive use of language: rhyme and scansion are not at all important. Suggestions are made in the Notes for ways of starting them off. They should also be encouraged to translate poems and stories which they may already know in their mother-tongue. This is an excellent way to improve their use of English. Nearly all the traditional poems in this book were translated by non-Africans. If teachers encourage their pupils to translate, it will not be necessary to go abroad for translations on future occasions!

5   Finally, a note on *rhythm*. The pupils may not find it at all easy to pick up the rhythms of English verse, because they transfer into spoken English the very different systems of stress which they know from their mother-tongues. They should be encouraged to pick up English rhythms in poetry, because it will help their use of spoken English. However, it is not much use teaching words like 'iambic' and 'trochaic'. By far the best way to learn is to find a poem with a strong rhythm (like No. 2 in this book)—and *clap*!

N.M.

1 Lullaby

A heart to hate you
Is as far as the moon.
A heart to love you
Is as near as the door.

Burundi

2 Peas and the rice

Peas and the *rice*,
Peas and the *rice*,
Peas and the *rice*, done,
Done, done, *done.*

New rice and *okra*,
Eat some and *left* some,
Peas and the *rice*, done,
Done, done, *done.*

U.S.A.

This is a sing-song *sound poem*. It should be read with claps
on the stressed syllables, like this:
(C = heavy clap c = light clap)

C	c	c	C	
Peas	and	the	rice	

C	c	c	C	
Peas	and	the	rice	

C	c	c	C	C
Peas	and	the	rice	done

C	C	C	
Done	done	done	

Write your own *sound-poem*, to be read out in class. It need
not have any more meaning than this one. You might also
like to make up a tune for it.

3

3 Tingalayo

Tingalayo!
Come, little donkey, *come*!
Tingalayo!
Come, little donkey, *come*!

My donkey *walk*, my donkey *talk*,
My donkey *eat* with a knife and *fork*,
My donkey *eat*, my donkey *sleep*,
My donkey *kick* with his two hind *feet*.

Tingalayo!
Come, little donkey, *come*!
Tingalayo!
Come, little donkey, *come*!

Trinidad

Another *sound-poem*, with a more complicated rhythm than the last one. Emphasise the stressed syllables by shouting or clapping. Try and *feel* the rhythm. (Note how the second verse has a different rhythm from the first one.)

How can you tell that the person talking to his donkey is not educated?

4 Chain-song

Ukwa killed Nwaka Dimkpolo
  E-e Nwaka Dimkpolo!
Who will punish this Ukwa for me?
  E-e Nwaka Dimkpolo!
Matchet will cut up this Ukwa for me
  E-e Nwaka Dimkpolo!
Who will punish this Matchet for me?
  E-e Nwaka Dimkpolo!
Blacksmith will hammer it for me
  E-e Nwaka Dimkpolo!
Who will punish this Blacksmith for me?
  E-e Nwaka Dimkpolo!
Fire will scorch this Blacksmith for me
  E-e Nwaka Dimkpolo!
Who will punish this Fire for me?
  E-e Nwaka Dimkpolo!
Water will quench this Fire for me
  E-e Nwaka Dimkpolo!
And who will punish this Water for me?
  E-e Nwaka Dimkpolo!
Earth will dry up this Water for me
  E-e Nwaka Dimkpolo!
Who will punish this Earth for me?
  E-e Nwaka Dimkpolo!
Earth will dry up this Water for me
  E-e Nwaka Dimkpolo-o-o-o!
What did Earth do?
  Earth swallowed Water
What did Water do?
  Water put out Fire
What did Fire do?
  Fire scorched Blacksmith
What did Blacksmith do?
  Blacksmith melted Matchet
What did Matchet do?

Matchet split Ukwa fruit
What did Ukwa do?
Ukwa fell on Nwaka Dimkpolo
  E-e Nwaka Dimkpolo!
Who will punish this Ukwa for me? . . .

Igbo

1 Why do you think this is called a 'chain-song'?
2 Write a 'chain-song' of your own, starting:
  'Bicycle pushed me into the ditch,
  Who will punish this bicycle for me? . . .'

5 Crooked song

I went into a crooked bush
And cut a crooked stick,
I stuck it by a crooked yam
And took a crooked hoe,
I dug the crooked yam again
And gave it to a crooked girl,
Who cooked it on a crooked fire
And gave it to a crooked man,
Who ate the crooked yam.

Igbo

1 Write a 'giant song', like this one but using the word
  'giant' in each line.
2 Illustrate the poem with a drawing or painting.

6 Mother Parrot's advice to her children

Never get up till the sun gets up,
Or the mists will give you a cold,
And a parrot whose lungs have once been touched
Will never live to be old.

Never eat plums that are not quite ripe,
For perhaps they will give you a pain;
And never dispute what the hornbill says,
Or you'll never dispute again.

Never despise the power of speech;
Learn every word as it comes,
For this is the pride of the parrot race,
That it speaks in a thousand tongues.

Never stay up when the sun goes down,
But sleep in your own home bed,
And if you've been good, as a parrot should,
You will dream that your tail is red.

A. K. Nyabongo
Ganda, trans.

1 What does the word 'touched' mean in the first verse?
   (Its use is explained by the other lines in the verse).
2 Explain line 8 'or you'll never dispute again.'
3 What is ridiculous about a parrot dreaming that his tail
   is red? (Line 16)
4 Write 'Mother Chicken's advice to her children' or 'Father
   Dog's advice to his children' (or any other animal).

Robert Kretschmer n. J. &.

7 You!

You!
Your head is like a hollow drum.
You!
Your eyes are like balls of flame.
You!
Your ears are like fans for blowing fire.
You!
Your nostril is like a mouse's hole.
You!
Your mouth is like a lump of mud.
You!
Your hands are like drum-sticks.
You!
Your belly is like a pot of bad water.
You!
Your legs are like wooden posts.
You!
Your backside is like a mountain-top.

Igbo

1 Add some more insults to this list.
2 Write a poem made up of compliments.

8 Chain-song (2)

If a jackal bothers you, show it a hyena,
If a hyena bothers you, show it a lion,
If a lion bothers you, show it an elephant,
If an elephant bothers you, show it a hunter,
If a hunter bothers you, show him a snake,
If a snake bothers you, show it a stick,
If a stick bothers you, show it a fire,
If a fire bothers you, show it a river,
If a river bothers you, show it the wind,
If the wind bothers you, show it God.

Fulani

Write your own chain-song, beginning:
'If a . . . bothers you, show it . . .'

9 The stem of the branch

None on earth is like her,
She that made me breathe.

None on earth is like her,
She that filled my stomach.

None on earth is like her,
She that knew why I cried.

None on earth is like her,
She that protected me.

None on earth is like her,
She that gave me my first lessons.

None on earth is like her,
She whose death orphans me.

L. M. Asiedu

1 What is the meaning of the poem's title?
2 Can you think of another title, using a different way of
   describing the mother and child?
3 How is the last verse different from the others?
4 Write a poem about a father, starting:
   'None on earth is like him . . .'

10 The poor mother

Another mother wishes you were hers,
But you are mine.
She wants to nurse you on her gorgeous rug,
She wishes you were hers,
To lay you on her rug of camel-hair,
But you are mine, to lay on my poor ragged mat.
She wishes you were hers, but you are mine!

Akan

1 How can you tell that the mother is poor (apart from the title)?
2 Would you describe the mother as humble or proud (or perhaps a mixture of the two)?
3 Is it a good thing for a poor mother to give her child to a rich person, say a relation, to bring up?

11 Lullaby

Sleep, sleep, little one, close your eyes, sleep,
 little one!
The night comes down, the hour has come,
 tomorrow it will be day.
Sleep, sleep, little one! On your closed eyes day
 has fled.
You are warm. You have drunk, sleep, sleep,
 little one!
Sleep, tomorrow you will be big, you will be
 strong.
Sleep, tomorrow you will take the bow and the
 knife.
Sleep, you will be strong, you will be straight,
 and I bent.
Sleep, tomorrow it is you, but it is mother always.

Gabon

This poem should be read so that the listener falls asleep by
the end of it!

1 Is the 'little one' a boy or a girl?—see lines 5 & 6.
2 What makes this poem 'sleepy'?
3 Explain the meaning of 'day has fled' in line 3.
4 How does the mother express her thoughts about
 growing old? (Note that the 'tomorrow' in the fifth line
 does not mean the very next day!)

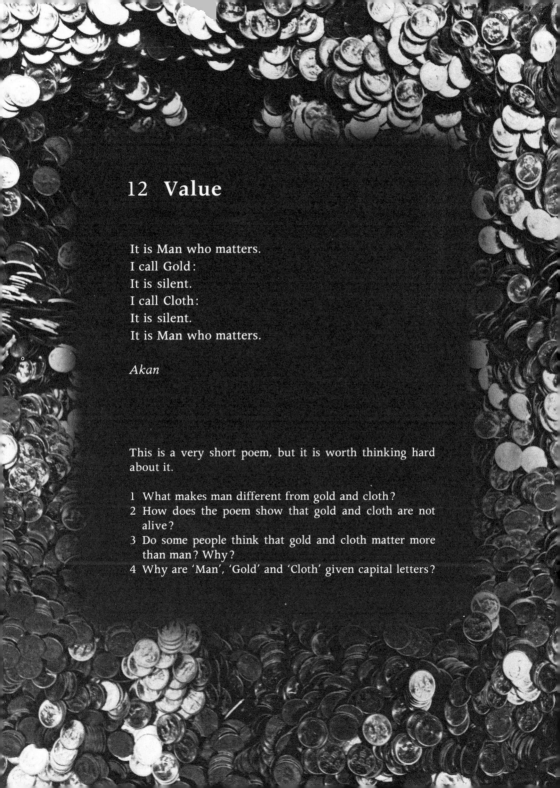

12 Value

It is Man who matters.
I call Gold:
It is silent.
I call Cloth:
It is silent.
It is Man who matters.

Akan

This is a very short poem, but it is worth thinking hard about it.

1 What makes man different from gold and cloth?
2 How does the poem show that gold and cloth are not alive?
3 Do some people think that gold and cloth matter more than man? Why?
4 Why are 'Man', 'Gold' and 'Cloth' given capital letters?

13 Busy

I've got some dust in my eye,
A crocodile's biting my leg,
A goat's got into the garden,
There's a porcupine in the cooking-pot,
The corn is drying on the rock,
The Chief has called me to court,
I have to go to my mother-in-law's funeral,
I'm busy!

Mbundu

1 What does the poem tell you about where the writer lives, and how he works?
2 Can you add some more lines which will make him even busier?
3 Write another 'Busy' poem about the things in your life which make you busy.

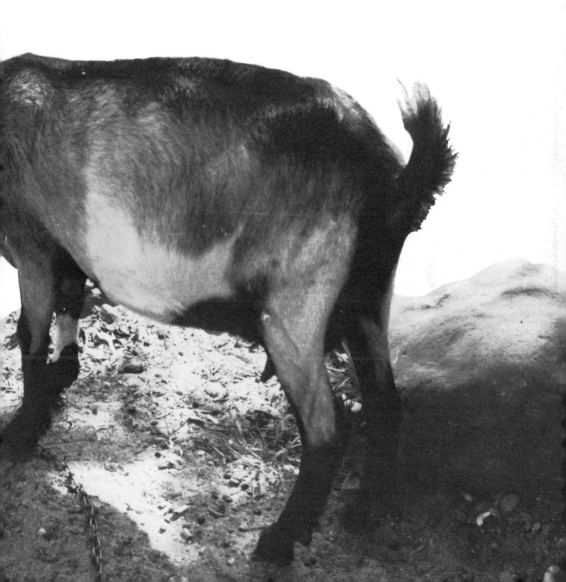

14 Drum-song

The blind man's stew is a black stew, a stew of
tears.

Mossi

This is called 'Drum-song' because it was originally played
on the talking-drum.
It is only a one-line poem, but it tells you more about what
it is like to be blind than a much longer poem might.
1 Is the 'stew' a real stew? What is it?
2 Write a one-line poem called 'The deaf man'.

15 Love-song

All things in nature love each other:
The lips love the teeth,
The beard loves the chin,
And all the little insects go *brrrrrr* together.

Soga

1 How do the 'lips love the teeth' and the 'beard love the chin'?

2 What other things 'love each other' like this?

3 Write a four-line poem like this one, but starting:
'Some things in nature hate each other . . .'

16 Song of the animal world

SOLOIST   The fish goes . . .   (Chorus) Hip!
The bird goes . . .   Viss!
The monkey goes . . .   Gnan!

FISH   I start to the left,
I twist to the right,
I am the fish
That slips through the water,
That slides,
That twists,
That leaps!

SOLOIST   Everything lives,
Everything dances,
Everything sings:
The fish goes . . .   (Chorus) Hip!
The bird goes . . .   Viss!
The monkey goes . . .   Gnan!

BIRD   The bird flies away,
       Flies, flies, flies,
       Goes, returns, passes,
       Climbs, floats, swoops.
       I am the bird!

SOLOIST   Everything lives,
          Everything dances,
          Everything sings:
          The fish goes . . .   (Chorus)   Hip!
          The bird goes . . .   Viss!
          The monkey goes . . .   Gnan!

MONKEY   The monkey! From branch to
             branch
         Runs, hops, jumps,
         With his wife and baby,
         Mouth stuffed full, tail in air,
         Here's the monkey! Here's the
             monkey!

SOLOIST   Everything lives,
          Everything dances,
          Everything sings:
          The fish goes . . .   (Chorus)   Hip!
          The bird goes . . .   Viss!
          The monkey goes . . .   Gnan!

                                              Zaire

This poem must be acted like a play, imitating the actions
of the animals mentioned.
Note that the sounds 'Hip! Viss! Gnan!' represent the *move-
ment* of the animals, *not* their voices.
If possible, study the movement of these animals in real life,
through observation.
This and many of the poems following are about the animal
world. They show that poetry and biology are not always
far apart. They both need *very close observation*.

22

17 Elephant

Elephant, death-bringer!
Elephant, spirit of the bush!
  With his one hand he brings two trees to the ground.
If he had two hands, he would tear the sky like an
      old rag.
Spirit who eats dog!
Spirit who eats ram!
Spirit who eats palm-fruit, thorns and all!
With four pestle-legs he flattens the grass,
Where he walks, the grass cannot stand again.
An elephant is no load for an old man—
Not even for a young man!

Yoruba

This poem must strike terror into the listener!

1 What is the elephant's 'one hand'?
2 How are his legs like pestles?
3 Can you add more lines to tell more about the elephant's
    frightening strength?

18 Hare

Son of the little dark-brown one with spots,
Little yellow one, leaper from the stubble,
Yonder is the son of the little dark-brown one,
Leaper from the treeless plain,
Leaper from the trunks of trees,
He leaps up, stiffens his tail,
And puts his ears back on his shoulders.

Hurutshe

This must be read in a quick, light voice, to suit the character
of the hare—in strong contrast with the previous poem.
If you don't know what 'stubble' means, look it up in a
dictionary.

1 How can you tell that the poem is about a young hare,
  and that a young hare is a different colour from an old
  one?
2 Have you seen a hare? If so, does the poem describe it
  well? Does it leave anything out?

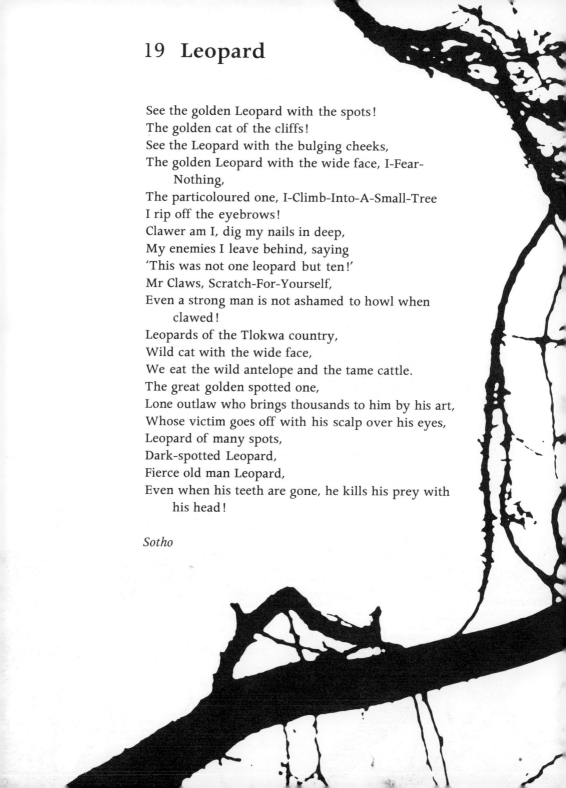

19 Leopard

See the golden Leopard with the spots!
The golden cat of the cliffs!
See the Leopard with the bulging cheeks,
The golden Leopard with the wide face, I-Fear-
    Nothing,
The particoloured one, I-Climb-Into-A-Small-Tree
I rip off the eyebrows!
Clawer am I, dig my nails in deep,
My enemies I leave behind, saying
'This was not one leopard but ten!'
Mr Claws, Scratch-For-Yourself,
Even a strong man is not ashamed to howl when
    clawed!
Leopards of the Tlokwa country,
Wild cat with the wide face,
We eat the wild antelope and the tame cattle.
The great golden spotted one,
Lone outlaw who brings thousands to him by his art,
Whose victim goes off with his scalp over his eyes,
Leopard of many spots,
Dark-spotted Leopard,
Fierce old man Leopard,
Even when his teeth are gone, he kills his prey with
    his head!

Sotho

This leopard should be even more terrifying than the
elephant in poem 16.
Look up 'particoloured' in a dictionary (though you may be
able to guess it).

1 Explain line 9 and line 17 (look up 'outlaw' if necessary)
2 Notice how the word 'Leopard' is repeated many times
  for emphasis—what other words are repeated for similar
  effect?

20 Pig

Pig that runs about busily,
Along the narrow paths, along the ground,
The sun shines, the pig grows fat.
Beast who grows fat in the sunlight,
Pig who runs about busily,
With little horns in his mouth.

Sotho

This vivid 'word-picture' describes how a pig only has time
for eating and getting fat!

Can you draw a word-picture of a goat, or a cock, in six
lines? What do *they* do?

21 Crocodile

Cruel one, killer while laughing,
Crocodile is the laughing teeth that kill.

Zulu

1 Why is the crocodile described as 'laughing'?
2 How does the poem make the crocodile seem so especially cruel?
3 Write an animal-poem in two lines. Try and use some words which *sound* like the animal as well as describing it.

22 Spider (1)

I'm told that the spider
Has coiled up inside her
Enough silky material
To spin an aerial
One-way track
To the moon and back;
Whilst I
Cannot even catch a fly.

Frank Collymore

When you read this poem, notice how the lines *rhyme* with
each other.

1 Do you prefer lines which rhyme? Why?
2 What does 'aerial' mean?
3 Lines 5 and 6 contradict each other—how?
4 What makes you think that the poet is not being very
   serious?

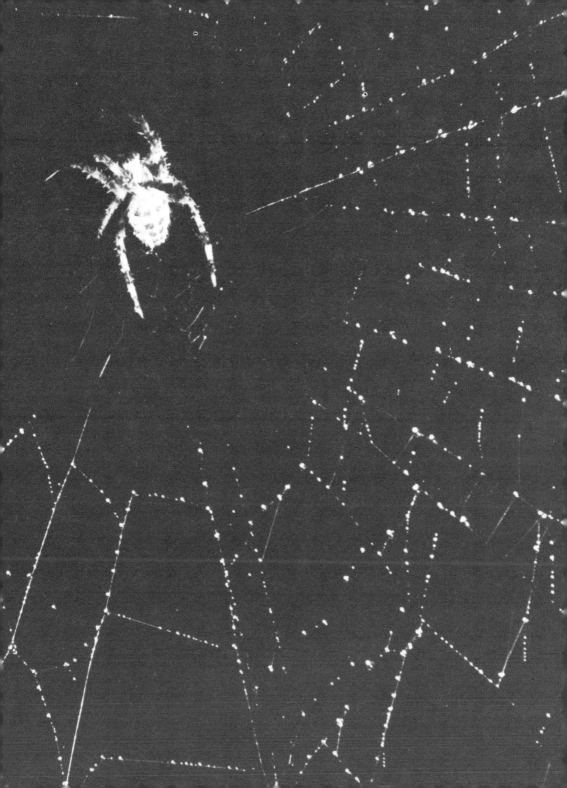

23 Spider (2)

Slow
As a limping cow
Or a mighty bull
With its legs split in two,
A great black spider comes out of the earth,
And climbs up the wall,
Then painfully sets his back against the trees,
Throws out his threads for the wind to carry,
Weaves a web that reaches the sky
And spreads his nets across the blue. . . .

Jean-Joseph Rabearivelo

1 Why is the spider like a bull 'with its legs split in two'
  (line 4)?
2 Compare this with the previous poem. How do the two
  poems differ from each other? Which do you prefer and
  why?
3 Which poem tells you more about spiders?

24 Lapobo

Lapobo,
Tall but not too tall,
Short but not too short,
She is of medium size.

Lapobo,
Her teeth are not as ash
Nor the colour of maize flour,
Her teeth are white as fresh milk.
The whiteness of her teeth
When I think of her
Makes food drop from my hand.

Lapobo,
Black but not too black,
Brown but not too brown,
Her skin colour is just between black and brown.

Lapobo,
Her heels have no cracks,
Her palms are smooth and tender to touch,
Her eyes—Ho! They can destroy anybody.

A. R. Cliff-Lubwa P'Chong

1 What other things might you compare Lapobo's teeth to?
2 Explain lines 9—11.
3 Explain the last line. What would you compare Lapobo's
  eyes to?
4 How does the writer tell us that he loves Lapobo?

25 Old Doc Hare

An old Hare lived in a house on a hill,
One hundred years old and never was ill;
His ears so long and his eyes so big,
And his legs so spry that he danced a jig;
He lived so long that he knew everything
About the beasts that walk and the birds that sing—
             This old Doc Hare,
             Who lived up there
In a mighty fine house on a mighty high hill.

He was doctor for all the beasts and birds—
He put on his specs and he used big words,
He felt the pulse, then he looked mighty wise,
He pulled out his watch and he shut both eyes;
He grabbed up his hat and he grabbed up his cane,
Then—'blam' went the door—he was gone like a
     train,
             This old Doc Hare,
             Who lived up there
In a mighty fine house on a mighty high hill.

Mister Bear fell sick—they sent for Doc Hare,
'Oh, Doctor, come quick, and see Mr Bear;
He's mighty near dead just as sure as you're born!
Too much of young pig, too much of green corn.
As he put on his hat, said old Doc Hare:
'I'll take along my lance and lance Mister Bear
             Said old Doc Hare,
             Who lived up there
In a mighty fine house on a mighty high hill.

Mister Bear he groaned, Mister Bear he growled,
While the old Mrs Bear and the children howled,
Doctor Hare took out his sharp little lance,
And pierced Mister Bear till it made him prance,

33

Then he grabbed up his hat and grabbed up his
    cane—
'Blam' went the door, he was gone like a train,
        This old Doc Hare,
        Who lived up there
In a mighty fine house on a mighty high hill.

But the very next day Mister Bear was dead;
When they told Doc Hare, he just scratched his
    head:
'If persons get well, or persons get worse,
Money's got to come into old Hare's purse;
Not for what folks do, but for what they *know*
Do the folks get paid'—and Hare laughed low,
        This smart old Hare,
        Who lived up there
In a mighty fine house on a mighty high hill!

James Edwin Campbell

This poem was written by an American, who based it on a
story he heard as a child. Comic stories about hares, rabbits,
tortoises and spiders are almost as common amongst
Americans of African descent as they are in Africa (where
they came from in the first place).
Try to feel the regular rhythm in this poem, like this:
'An *old* Hare *lived* in a *house* on the *hill*,
One *hun*dred years *old* and *nev*er was *ill*;
His *ears* so *long* and his *eyes* so *big*,
And his *legs* so *spry* that he *danced* a *jig* . . .

1 What does 'spry' mean (line 4)? Even if you don't know,
  you can guess from the rest of the line—and the same
  with 'jig' in the same line.
2 Why did Mr Bear become ill?
3 Do you think Doc Hare was a good doctor?
4 Can you make up an animal story set in modern life—in
  a city, or a school?

26 Love song

Never shall I love with one who is a baby,
(Joy, joy, Mother, this one sleeps in innocence.)
Never shall I love with one who is no lover,
(Joy, joy, Mother, this one sleeps in innocence.)
I shall love with one who is strong and brave and
        handsome,
(Joy, joy, Mother, this one sleeps in innocence.)
I shall love with him who appears and causes
        heartaches,
(Joy, joy, Mother, this one sleeps in innocence.)
Yes, I will have a whirlwind of a man!
(Joy, joy, Mother, this one sleeps in innocence.)

Zulu

In this poem, you have to imagine a girl rocking her baby
sister to sleep—the baby is the 'one who sleeps in innocence'.
Each line has two main stresses, which gives it a rocking
rhythm:
Never shall I *love*/with one who is a *baby*,
(Joy, joy, *Moth*er,/this one sleeps in *inn*ocence)

What does the girl compare her lover to in line 9 and why
is it a suitable comparison?

27 Anti-love song

All right then, girl, refuse me!
The grains of maize you eat in your village are
      human eyes!
The tumblers from which you drink are human
      skulls!
The cassava roots you eat are human leg-bones!
The sweet potatoes are human fingers!
Very well then, girl, refuse me!

Thonga

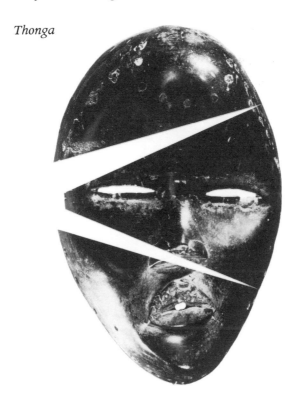

1 The speaker sounds as if he is telling the girl to refuse him.
   Is that really what he is doing?
2 Why does he talk in this way?
3 Do you think the poem is completely serious?

28 Wicked stepmother

My father, he married
A crocodile wife,
   She bites, she bites.
   Iya, Iyawoye!

Ndau

If you say the last line in a loud, complaining voice, you will
not have to ask what the words mean!
Do you think the speaker's father really married a crocodile?
If not, what does he (or she) mean by calling her a crocodile
and saying she bites?

29 Sound-pictures

k'we (A striking match)
gwengwendere (Enamel plates dropping)
nyiri nyiri nyiri (Light flickering on a cinema screen)
dhabhu dhabhu dhabhu (An eagle flying *slowly*)
go, go, go, ngondo ngondo ngondo, pkaka pkaka
     pkaka pkaka pkaka (A tree being felled, falling,
     and its branches splintering)
khwanya, khwanya, khwanya (A tortoise on the march)
pha-pha-pha-pha (Flight of the butterfly)
noni, noni, noni-djamaaa (A frog: three hops and a
     jump into the pond)
tlikwi-tlikwi (The drunkard's walk)
fambifa-fambifa-fambifa (A tired dog)
peswa-peswa (High-heeled shoes)

Shona & Thonga

Each line must be read so that it sounds like the meaning
in brackets.
If you can speak them so that a listener guesses their meaning
without looking at the page, you can be very proud of
yourself! Notice how some represent sounds, some sights,
and some movements.
Of course, these sound-pictures are not strictly poems, but
sound is an essential part of poetry—it helps to bring de-
scriptions to life.
Try inventing sound-pictures of your own. Write sounds to
represent the following:

    1 a car-engine starting up.
    2 rain falling on hard ground.
    3 wind amongst leaves.
    4 someone blowing his nose.
    5 a heavy rock being dropped into water.
    6 lightning and thunder.

You can think of many more yourself.

30 Yaa, the Adowa dancer

The tune of *Adowa*
Drives Yaa to frenzy,
Her legs alternate—
    they close,
    they cross,
    they open,
    they part.
Oh, what a dancer,
The dancer of *Adowa*.
Her trunk goes—
    to the left,
    to the right,
    to the front,
    to the back.
Oh what a dancer,
The dancer of *Adowa*.
Her hands move—
    Backwards,
    forwards,
    upwards,
    downwards.
Oh what a dancer,
The dancer of *Adowa*.
Her head turns—
    to the east,
    to the west,
    to the north,
    to the south.
Oh what a dancer,
The dancer of *Adowa*.

L. M. Asiedu

Adowa is the name of a Ghanaian dance.
This entire poem is a sound-picture, in which the movement
of the dance is suggested. It should be read so that the
listener feels that he can see the dance, and even wants to
take part in it himself or herself.

1 How is the rhythm of the dance suggested?
2 Describe a dance, either in poetry or prose, so that the
   reader (or listener) feels that he can hear the music and
   join in the dance.

31 Rain magic

Gentle breeze is the father of rain,
Soft wind is the father of cloudburst,
Rain will not drench me today;
Rain will pack its belongings and go away.
      The antelope is humming,
      The buffalo is grumbling,
      The pig grunts in its belly.
Words have angered the red monkey,
But today he was given the right words
And his anger will disappear.

Yoruba

1 This is a magic charm to keep the rain away. It contains
   metaphors which describe first the breeze before a storm,
   then distant thunder. What are these metaphors?
2 The 'red monkey' is a *personification* of the thunder-
   storm. What other personifications are there?
3 Describe a thunderstorm, using as many metaphors and
   similes ('*like* so-and-so') as possible.

32 A sudden storm

The wind howls, the trees sway,
The loose house-top sheets clatter and clang,
The open window shuts with a bang,
    And the sky makes night of the day.

Helter-skelter the parents run,
Pressed with a thousand minor cares:
'Hey, you there! pack the house-wares!
    And where on earth's my son?'

Home skip the little children:
'Where have you been, you naughty boy?'—
The child can feel nothing but joy,
    For he loves the approach of the rain.

The streets clear, the houses fill,
The noise gathers as children shout
To rival the raging wind without,
    And nought that can move is still—

A bright flash!—a lighted plain;
Then, from the once-black heavens,
Accompanied by noise that deafens,
    Steadily pours the rain.

Pious Oleghe

1 Pick out the words which give sound-pictures of the
  noises of the storm.
2 In what ways does this poem give a different idea of a
  thunderstorm from the previous poem?
3 How does this poet's language differ from that of the
  previous poet?

33 The warrior's return

He comes! He comes!
Striding along on camel-rug in triumph.
Yes, stranger, we are making ourselves ready!
Agyei the warrior is drunk—
The green mamba with the fearful eyes.
    Yes, Agyei the warrior,
      He strides along the camel-rug in triumph,
    Make way!

He comes! He comes!
Stamping on his prisoners like sandals.
Yes, stranger, we are making ourselves ready!
Adum Agyei is drunk,
The green mamba, *Afaafa Adu!*
    Yes, Agyei the warrior,
      He strides along the camel-rug in triumph.
    Make way!

Akan

This must be read in a bold, triumphant voice.

1 What words and phrases especially give an impression
  of Agyei's courage and magnificence?
2 Can you think of any more expressions to emphasise these
  qualities?
3 Who do you imagine is speaking these lines? Why is
  Agyei called 'stranger'?
4 Paint or draw a picture of Agyei.

34 Lucky old sun

Up in the morning,
Out on the job,
Work like the devil for my pay,
While that lucky old Sun
Has nothing to do
But roll around heaven all day!

Work for my woman,
Toil for my kids,
Sweat till I'm wrinkled and grey,
While that lucky old Sun
Has nothing to do
But roll around heaven all day!

Dear Lord above, can't you see I'm pining?
Tears roll in my eyes.
Bring down that cloud with the silver lining,
Take me to Paradise!

Show me that river,
Take me across,
Wash all my troubles away.
Like that lucky old Sun,
Give me nothing to do,
But roll around Heaven all day!

U.S.A.

The river in the last verse is the River Jordan, which
according to traditional Christian belief divides Earth from
Heaven.

1 The 'cloud with the silver lining' in the third verse is the
   same as in the proverb 'Every cloud has a silver lining'—
   what does it mean?

2 Which is the saddest verse and which is the happiest?
   Why?
3 What lines could be called a 'chorus'?
4 In what way does 'Heaven' in the last verse have a
   different meaning to that in the first two verses?

35 The foreigner

The foreigner,
Chin of a goat,
The foreigner comes strutting
With his red skin.

Sudan

1 Explain the second line.
2 Where do you think the foreigner comes from?
3 Write a poem like this, with four short lines, called
   'The Baby'.

36 Beggar

Beggar,
There he stoops all day,
Wrinkled,
Grey-haired,
Senile,
With his stained beard, and his pavement bowl,
Hand hopefully outstretched,
Entreating,
Entreating with his eyes,
Entreating with his tongue,
Entreating with his hand.

Yet we saunter by,
Eyes earthwards riveted.

Sometimes a gnarled stick,
Sometimes none,
Always the filthy *kanzu*,
The tattered *kanzu*,
We have observed him sightless,
Deaf and dumb,
We have seen him piteously, hopping
Hobbling and crawling.
Still we ignore the gnarled palm,
Still we pore over the drab pavement.

Perhaps he is blind
Pitiful
Yet he misses not every proffered coin
Though the gesture is silent.

Perhaps he can see?

So we stalk past.

A. Kassam

1 Look up 'senile' (line 5) and 'rivet' (line 13) in a dictionary.
  What does 'riveted' mean here?
2 What does 'pore over' mean (line 23)? Why do people
  'pore over the pavement' when they pass the beggar?
3 Make up a conversation between a blind beggar and a
  passer-by who believes the beggar can see.

37 Swing low

Swing low, sweet chariot,
Coming for to carry me home!
Swing low, sweet chariot,
Coming for to carry me home!

I looked over Jordan and what did I see?
Coming for to carry me home!
A band of angels coming after me,
Coming for to carry me home!

If you get there before I do,
Coming for to carry me home!
Tell all my friends I'm coming too,
Coming for to carry me home!

Swing low, sweet chariot,
Coming for to carry me home!
Swing low, sweet chariot,
Coming for to carry me home!

U.S.A.

This should be sung or read by a soloist, with the rest of
the class singing or saying the refrain:
'Coming for to carry me home!'

1 What is the 'home' referred to here?
2 What is this poem really about, in terms of everyday
   life?
3 Is it a cheerful or depressing poem? Give reasons.

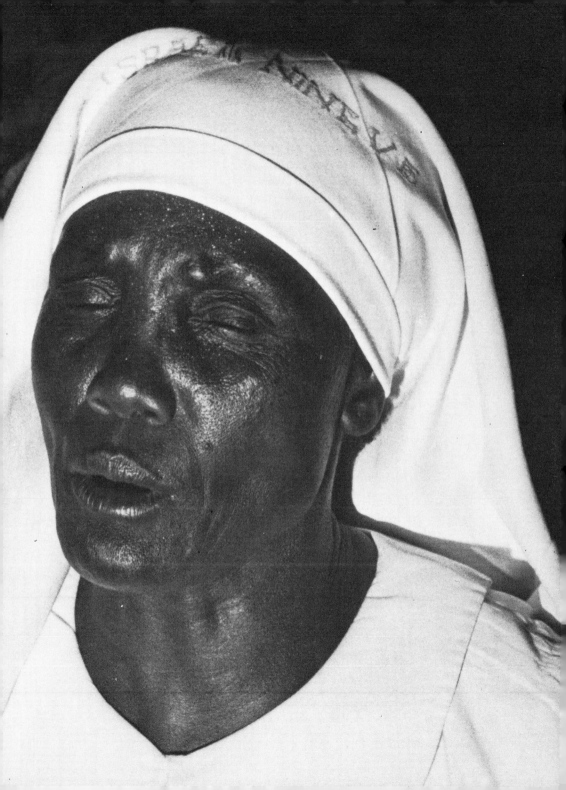

38 The cunjah man

O children, run, the Cunjah Man,
Him mouth as big as frying-pan,
Him ears am small, him eyes am red,
Him have no tooth in him old head,
Him have him roots, him work him trick,
Him roll him eye, him make you sick—
 The Cunjah Man, the Cunjah Man,
 O children, run, the Cunjah Man!

Him have a ball of red, red hair,
Him hide it under the kitchen stair,
Mam Jude, her pass along that way,
And now her have a snake, they say.
Him wrap around her body tight,
Her eyes pop out, a awful sight—
 The Cunjah Man, the Cunjah Man,
 O children, run, the Cunjah Man!

Miss Jane, her drive him from her door,
And now her hens won't lay no more;
The Jersey cow, her done fall sick,
It's all done by the Cunjah trick.
Him put a root under 'Lijah's bed,
And now the man, he sure am dead—
 The Cunjah Man, the Cunjah Man,
 O children, run, the Cunjah Man!

Me see him stand the other night,
Right in the road in white moon-light;
Him toss him arms, him whirl him round,
Him stomp him foot upon the ground;
The snakes come crawling, one by one,
Me hear them hiss, me break and run—
 The Cunjah Man, the Cunjah Man,
 O children, run, the Cunjah Man!

James Edwin Campbell

1 In what ways do you think the poet shows how people who believed in the Cunjah Man's powers were slightly ridiculous?
2 Write out the poem in correct English. What does this do to the feeling of the poem?
3 Draw a picture illustrating the poem, making the Cunjah Man fit the description in verse 1.

39 Long John

With his shiny blade,
Got it in his hand,
Going to chop out the live oaks
That are in this land.
He's Long John,
He's long gone,
He's gone, gone,
Like a turkey in the corn,
With his long clothes on,
He's Long John,
He's long gone,
He's gone,
He's gone.

U.S.A.

This is a very simple sound-poem—almost a nonsense-poem; but it can be read so as to fill the listener with sadness about Long John who's long gone.
The poem tells you very little about Long John. Can you imagine some more about his life, what he looked like, what happened to him, etc.?

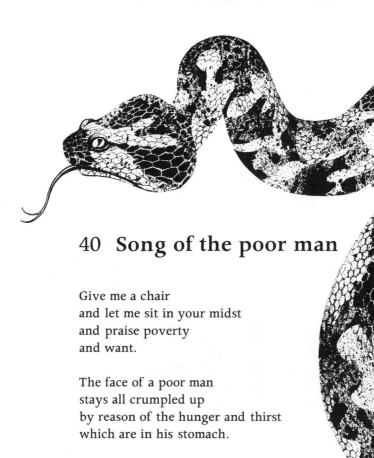

40 Song of the poor man

Give me a chair
and let me sit in your midst
and praise poverty
and want.

The face of a poor man
stays all crumpled up
by reason of the hunger and thirst
which are in his stomach.

A poor man knows not
how to eat with a rich man.
When he starts eating fish
he eats its head.

Go and invite him
who has no bread
to come and eat crumbs
and thorns in the platters.

A poor man is nobody
because he has nothing.
Though nobly born
he is granted no favour.

A poor man is a snake—
his brothers avoid him
because of the misery
of the poverty-stricken.

But when a poor man is ill,
it leads his people
to show him kindness;
when a rich man is ill,
to light a lamp
he must wait for a slave.

Zanzibar

It may seem odd that anyone should 'praise poverty'
(verse 1), and in fact much of this poem is not at all in praise
of poverty.

1 Do you think there is anything good about poverty?
2 Can you think of any reasons for praising it, beside those
given by this poor man?
3 Can you think of any reasons for cursing riches?
4 Write a 'Song of the rich man', in four-line verses like
this one.

54

41 Streamside exchange

CHILD   River bird, river bird,
           Sitting all day long
           On hook over grass,
           River bird, river bird,
           Sing to me a song
           Of all that pass
           And say,
           Will mother come back today?

BIRD   You cannot know
           And should not bother;
           Tide and market come and go
           And so has your mother.

John Pepper Clark

This is another poem with simple words but difficult
meaning.

1 Is the river bird's answer comforting, or saddening?
  Perhaps the author means it to be mystifying, like
  asking advice from your own reflection in a mirror.
  Try and make up your own mind what it means.
2 How would you answer the child?
3 The 'hook' in line 3 is a branch, on which the bird sits.
  Why does the poet use this word?

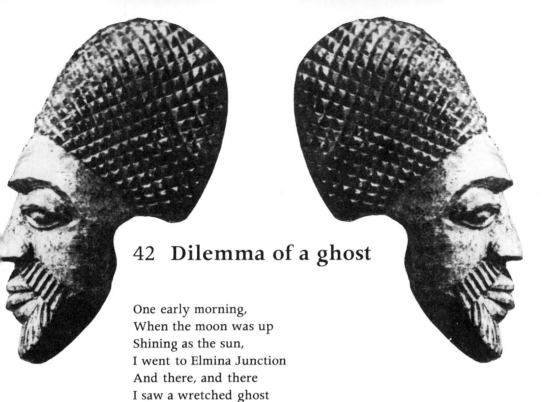

42 Dilemma of a ghost

One early morning,
When the moon was up
Shining as the sun,
I went to Elmina Junction
And there, and there
I saw a wretched ghost
Going up and down
Singing to himself:
    'Shall I go
    To Cape Coast,
    Or to Elmina?
    I don't know,
    I can't tell.
    I don't know,
    I can't tell.'

Ama Ata Aidoo

1 Guess what 'Dilemma' means by reading the poem, and
  then look it up in a dictionary to see if you were right.
2 Elmina and Cape Coast are two towns near each other in
  Ghana. What is a junction? Why is it suitable that the
  ghost should be at a junction?
3 What does this poem tell us about making up one's mind?

43 Madam and her madam

I worked for a woman,
She wasn't mean —
But she had a twelve-room
House to clean.

Had to get breakfast,
Dinner, and supper too—
Then take care of her children
When I got through.

Wash, iron, and scrub,
Walk the dog around—
It was too much,
Nearly broke me down.

I said, 'Madam,
Can it be
You're trying to make a
Pack-horse out of me?'

She opened her mouth.
She cried, 'Oh, no!
You know, Alberta,
I love you so!'

I said, 'Madam,
That may be true—
But I'll be dogged
If I love you!'

Langston Hughes

The last two lines show, with the use of the slang phrase
'I'll be dogged', that under no circumstances whatever can
the servant bring herself to love her mistress.

1 What is the name of the 'Madam' who tells this story?
2 What sort of person is she?
3 Compare this with Poem 36. Which seems more true to
   life? How are they different in the way they show
   poverty?
4 Imagine what 'Madam's madam' says in reply to the last
   verse, and how the conversation goes on.

44 Riddles

The black one is squatting—the red one is licking
    his bottom.
(Cooking-pot and fire)

Two tiny birds jump over two hundred trees.
    (Eyes)

The mourner has stopped weeping.
The pitying friend is still crying.
    (Rain and the dripping leaves after rain)

A round calabash amongst the spear-grass.
    (Moon and Stars)

We invited him to come and warm himself in the
    sun—he came.
But when we asked him to take his bath, he said
    that his death had come.
    (Salt)

Yoruba

These riddles are so hard that you will be extremely clever
to guess them, and may take a little time to realise how they
fit their meaning!
Note that all these riddles are in fact *metaphors*—they
describe one thing in terms of another.
Make up riddles of your own, to ask each other.

45 Upside-down cake

I am going to make
An upside-down cake.
I know I'll need some flour,
But I'm going to wait
At least half an hour
Before I begin to bake.

I'll need some fat
And eggs, and water,
Sugar in an upside-down bowl
And mix all of that.

Before I can really begin
I'll need an upside-down tin,
And an upside-down oven
To fit everything in.

I know you will say
I will have to stand on my head
To eat an upside-down cake.
But I have thought of that:
I will choke and be dead.

So I will change my mind
And bake instead
A sideways cake
And eat it
Sideways in bed.

I. Choonara

This shows how a good nonsense-poem has to contain quite
a lot of sense!
Draw a picture to go with this poem.

46 Western civilization

Sheets of tin nailed to posts
driven in the ground
make up the house.

Some rags complete
the intimate landscape.

The sun slanting through cracks
welcomes the owner

After twelve hours of slave
labour.
breaking rock
shifting rock
breaking rock
shifting rock
fair weather
wet weather
breaking rock
shifting rock

Old age comes early.

A mat on dark nights
is enough when he dies
gratefully
of hunger.

Agostinho Neto
trans. Margaret Dickinson

1 Explain the title. What is civilization? Is the poet really describing civilization?
2 What does 'intimate' mean (line 5)? Why does the poet use the word here?
3 How does the poet suggest the unpleasantness of the man's life?
4 Why does the poet use the word 'gratefully' in line 21? Is the man really grateful?
5 Write a poem or prose passage describing the kind of life which the man would like to live.

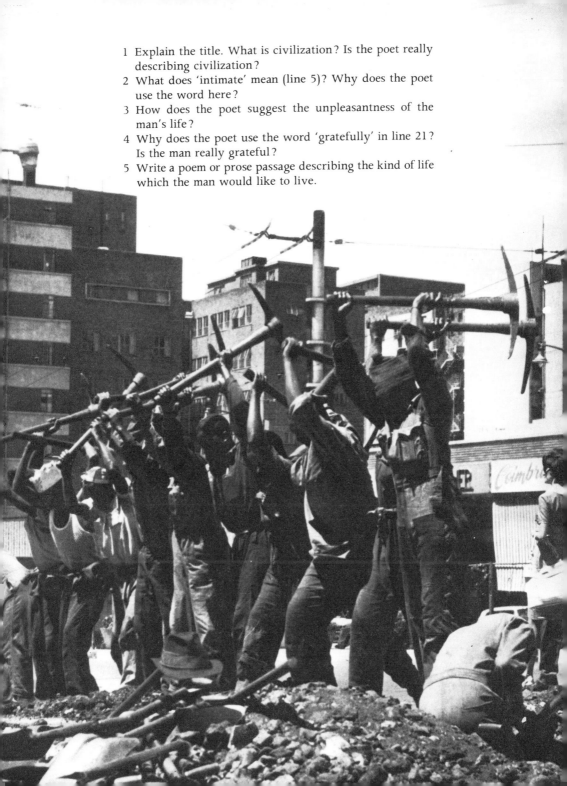

47 Beauty

He who meets beauty and does not look at it will
     soon be poor:
Red feathers are the pride of the parrot,
Young leaves are the pride of the palm-tree,
White flowers are the pride of the leaves,
A well-swept verandah is the pride of the
     householder,
A straight tree is the pride of the forest,
The fast deer is the pride of the bush,
The rainbow is the pride of heaven,
A beautiful woman is the pride of her husband,
Children are the pride of their mother,
The moon and stars are the pride of the sun,
Beauty and good luck are on their way!

Yoruba

1 Do you believe what the first line says? How would you
explain it?
2 Add some more lines in the same form: ' . . . is the pride
of the . . .', about other beautiful things.
3 What do we mean when we call things beautiful?

48 Palm leaves of childhood

When I was very small indeed,
And Joe and Fred were six-year giants,
My father, they and I, with soil
Did mix farm-yard manure.
In this we planted coconuts,
Naming them by brothers' names.
The palms grew faster far than I,
And soon, ere I could grow a Man,
They, flowering, reached their goal!
Like the ear-rings that my sister wore
Came the tender golden flowers.
I watched them grow from gold to green;
The nuts as large as Tata's head.
I craved the milk I knew they bore.
I listened to the whispering leaves,
When night winds did wake.
They haunt me still in work and play:
Those whispering leaves behind the slit
On the cabin wall of childhood's
Dreaming and becoming.

G. Adali-Mortti

1 Why does the writer call Joe and Fred 'giants' (line 2)?
  Who do you think they were?
2 In what way is the writer comparing the coconuts with
  himself and his brothers and sisters?
3 Who do you think Tata was (line 13)?
4 Where was the poet when he heard the whispering of
  the palm-leaves (lines 18, 19)?
5 Write a poem or prose passage about your own childhood.
6 Do you think this poem was written by a child? Give
  reasons.

49 In the beginning

In the beginning
God made the earth,
After that he took two stones and made them into
      Sun and Moon.
He further created Rain,
Whose desire was to fall down and cover the earth
      with water,
And Darkness, over whom Moon scattered a
      basketful of seeds,
Which were the Stars.

There were no people on the earth at first,
So God made Kiyomba, a man, and two wives.
One wife was a young woman,
The other, Kizumu, a snake.

Kizumu gave her co-wife two fruits,
Saying: 'Give one to our husband, and eat them
      together,
Only remember: do not eat the fruit on the way!'
But the young wife was curious,
On the way, she opened the fruit to see what was
      inside.
Inside was a powder,
It made the young woman ashamed,
She knew she was a woman and her husband a man.
After Kiyomba had eaten the fruit, they started to
      quarrel.

God gave Kiyomba some seeds,
Kiyomba plaited them into his hair,
When he reached home he spread the seeds on the
      ground.
All fruits and vegetables grew from them.

God gave Kiyomba two baskets,
Saying: 'One is for you, and one for Kizumu the
    snake:
Choose which you want.'
Kiyomba's basket was heavy,
He opened it,
It held Death.
Kizumu opened her basket,
It held Life,
It taught her to change her skin like a cloth when
    it grew old.

God was angry with Kiyomba for choosing Death,
He left the earth and went off up to heaven.
Kiyomba was sad without God,
He longed to be with him again,
Together with his wife, he set off to find God,
Walking towards the horizon, to where the sky
    rests on bronze columns,
Towards the country where the sun sets.
But they never reached the place of their desire,
And on the way they had many children
Who filled the earth with people.

God said to Kiyomba:
'As long as you are on earth you cannot join me,
But look! I have made a new thing:
It is called Soul,
It will be the kernel of life for you.
I will also give you sticks to rub together,
To make fire,
I will give you a spear to hunt with,
The hoe to dig and make farms,
And finally I give you all the fruits of the earth;
You may eat them all but one—
That which is called Banana,
That you may not eat.'

But Woman, Kiyomba's wife, picked some bananas
And ate them.
Very soon, God saw that some bananas were
      missing,
He called his four children together—
Sun, Moon, Man and Woman,
'I will bury you all,' he told them,
'But the one who did not steal will rise again
      afterwards.'
So he buried them.
The first to rise was the Sun,
After only one night, he rose up out of the earth;
Then, four days afterwards, Moon arose in the sky,
At first she was thin and slender, but steadily she
      grew.
After these two, no-one arose,
The first Man and the first Woman remained buried,
And buried they remain to the present day.

Only *Mutima*, the Soul, was taken to heaven by
      God,
Because it was his youngest creation,
And he loved it dearly.

Baluba

1 In what direction (north, south, east or west) did Kiyomba
  and his wife walk to find God?
2 What is a 'kernel'? (Line 47) How is Soul like a kernel?
3 Explain the description of the moon (Line 67).
4 What does this Creation story have in common with
  those which you already know, in the Bible or the Koran?
  What do you think are the most important differences?

50 Signature

I am an honest African,
Do not think of me otherwise.
I am not of mixed lineage,
Neither on my mother's nor my father's side.
However fine other lineage may be,
I am not sprung from it.
I am no Arab nor a European,
I am not of Indian descent.
I tell this to the world
So that the curious may know.

Shabban Robert

Teacher's Notes

1   A very simple poem to start with. Get several pupils to read it out, emphasising the warm, loving feeling. It will help if they emphasise the words *far* and *near* in contrast to each other.

Note that the poem is in two balanced parts. Show this to the class by getting one person to read the first two lines and another the second two. Ask them to write out the same poem, but with a different suitable word instead of *moon* in line 2, and another for *door* in line 4.

2   This is a *sound-poem*: it has very little meaning, but a very strong rhythm. I have pointed out in the Introduction that pupils often find it difficult to pick up the rhythm of English poetry. This is a very good example to practise with. Get the class to clap together, four beats to a line, with very strong emphasis on the first and third claps (*Clap* clap, *Clap* clap), while reading the poem. At the same time, they can *shout* the emphasised words ('*Peas* and the *rice*').

This method can be used with many other poems in the anthology, especially Nos. 3, 5, 25, and 26.

If they can make up a tune for the poem, or a clapping dance, they will see how close poetry can be to music. Get them to write their own 'nonsense verse', to be clapped out in the same way.

3   A slightly more difficult 'sound-poem', which needs the same treatment as the last one.

Point out the bad grammar in the second verse, and ask whether a poet should always use 'good English', or whether it depends who is supposed to be speaking in the poem.

4   This should be read by dividing the class into two

soloists and a chorus, with one soloist asking the questions, the other answering and the chorus saying the 'E-e Nwaka Dimkpolo!' lines.

The pupils can use another name—perhaps someone they know—instead of Nwaka Dimkpolo.

Some pupils may know chain-songs like this themselves, perhaps in their mother-tongue. If so, ask them to translate these into English on the blackboard, and let the class recite them.

5   Another song for clapping:
    'I *went* into a *crook*ed bush
    And *cut* a crooked *stick*' etc.
It can also be used as a mime-play, with a chorus saying the words, and individuals acting out the parts of the speaker, the crooked girl and the crooked man.

6   A poem with a strong regular rhythm, suitable for clapping:
    '*Nev*er get *up* till the *sun* gets *up*,
    Or the *mists* will *give* you a *cold*,
    And a *par*rot whose *lungs* have *once* been *touched*
    Will *never live* to be *old*.'—and so on.
Notice how the rhymes in the second and fourth lines of each verse, and the internal rhyme 'good/ should' in Line 15, add to the regular beat. The poem should be clapped through several times to get a feel for the rhythm.

It is also very suitable for practice in clear speaking. Get pupils to take one verse each, pronouncing the words very clearly, and at the same time remembering to keep the suitable expression for a parent giving her children good advice.

7   Get the class to say the short ('you!') lines together; individual pupils can read out the descriptive lines. This is a good opportunity to show how important comparisons (or similes) are in poetry. How boring this

poem would be if it just said 'Your head is empty, your eyes are red, your ears are big', etc. By using interesting comparisons, it wakes up our imagination. Pupils can be encouraged to develop their ability to make interesting comparisons, by playing the following game in class. One pupil things of an object, and the other pupils try and think of comparisons which the object fits. For example:

'This ruler is like . . .'
    'A straight road.'
    'A narrow bridge.'
    'An aeroplane wing.' etc.

The pupil who makes the best comparison (in the teacher's judgement) suggests the next object.

8   The class will enjoy making up a chain-song together, as suggested in the Pupils' Note, which can be written up on the blackboard as they compose it. Let them decide amongst themselves which are the best suggestions for each line. If they can't think of an opening line, try: 'If a rat bothers you, show it a cat'.

9   After getting the class to read the poem (perhaps one pupil, one verse), make sure they know what it is about.

Then ask them to explain the title, which is more difficult than the poem. Explain that it is really a comparison (comparing the child and mother to the stem and the branch), although it does not use 'like'. In other words, it is a metaphor. This poem, like all the previous ones, uses repetition. Compare it with poems 5 and 6, and discuss how repetition has a completely different effect in each poem.

10   The poem should be read with a great feeling of maternal tenderness. In a few lines, the poem tells a story of two different mothers which could well be made into a play in three scenes:

Scene 1: The poor mother talks to her baby, telling it that although she finds life difficult, she will never let the baby leave her.

Scene 2: The rich woman comes and argues that she should have the child.

Scene 3: They take the child to a wise uncle or aunt, who decides which of them should keep it. (Characters such as husband, neighbours, etc. can be added).

11 You may have to explain that the lullaby was written by hunting people, which is why the boy will 'take the bow and the knife' when he grows up. *Sleep* is a long, soft, restful word. Make pupils practise saying the word, making it as 'sleepy' as they can. Tell them to emphasise it wherever it occurs in the poem. Ask them to think of other words which sound 'sleepy' — 'soft', 'quiet', 'still', etc. Then use them in a poem of four lines which will send the listener to sleep!

12 This shows that a short poem with simple words may express difficult and important thoughts — though poetry teachers should *not* give their pupils the idea that a poem is good just because it is simple or complicated! Show how the poem has a simple but effective 'sandwich' pattern: the first and last lines are the same, and the middle pairs of lines echo each other. Many poems have a regular shape, for example Nos. 1, 2, 3 and 9, which can be compared with this one, and the pupils can be asked to point out the shape. This poem can be read in a dramatic way.
The reader should pause after 'I call Gold', as if waiting for an answer, and the same with 'I call Cloth'.

13 This is an excellent starting-point for pupils to write their own poems, following the suggestion in Pupils' Note 3. They can either do this individually out of

class or collectively in class, with each pupil suggesting one line.

Ask the class what gives this poem shape. In this case, there is no exact repetition, but each line is about something urgent that is happening.

14 One of the uses of poetry is to make us know how other people feel. Although it is easy to *feel* the sense of the line, it is not so easy to explain exactly what the 'stew' is. Does it describe the blind-man's world, or does the line mean that a blind man cannot see what he eats? Again, does the 'stew of tears' mean that he drinks his own tears?

Poetry often says many things at the same time. That is one of the differences between poetry and prose.

Point out that mentioning stew makes the poem sadder because we usually think of stew as something cheerful.

Ask the class to cover their eyes and imagine they are blind. Make them describe what the world seems like now.

15 This is not the usual kind of love-song, about love between man and woman.

Ask the class what 'love' means, and what different meanings it can have.

16 This poem must be made into a dramatic performance by dividing the class, and making different sections take the part of the various animals. Pupils should be encouraged to exercise their powers of observation, and imitation is a very effective way of doing this. This poem and the other animal poems which follow, will give plenty of opportunity.

These animal poems should be compared and contrasted with each other. Nearly all are suitable for dramatic performance. They are also suitable for painting and drawing. The poetry teacher and art teacher can consult about this: it is a good way of showing that school subjects are not really as separate from each other as the time-table makes them.

17 (See previous note.)
Point out that the simile in line 4, 'tear the sky like an old rag', is particularly effective because it expresses a rather abstract idea in terms of something familiar and real ('an old rag'). In reality, an elephant would never be able to tear the sky. Poetry very often tells us things which are not literally true, but which are true to our *feeling*.
The last two lines may at first sight seem so obvious that they are not worth saying, so help the class to discuss what they make us *feel* about the elephant.

18 Get the class to describe a dog, so that someone who has never seen a dog would know what it looks like. This can be done in two stages: first describe *everything* about the dog, and then write only seven lines which select the *most important* things about the dog (as is done in this poem).

19 In some parts of the poem, the leopard is treated as if it were a human being. Look for examples with the class (e.g. lines 10 and 16) considering whether it makes them think of the leopard as an animal or as a human being.
Ask them in what ways human beings can be like leopards.
Make them choose seven words from the poem which especially express the leopard's fierceness.
Subject for a story: 'My meeting with a leopard'.

20 Get the class to choose the words in the poem which express the pig's appearance and movement. If necessary, explain with the help of a picture how the 'little horns' refers to the tusks of a wild pig. Let them find other words which would describe the pig.

21 A good example with which to discuss the *sound* of words. Ask the class to pick out words with 'k' sounds. If they put them together and speak them with emphasis: 'Cruel *k*iller *c*ro*c*odile *k*ill' they will hear how hard and harsh the *k* sound can be—like the crocodile itself.

These are examples of *sound* echoing the *sense*: something which brings imaginary things to life in poetry.

Ask the class to think of other words in which the sound echoes the sense (e.g. *puff, growl, whistle, bubble*). They may know several words of this kind in their mother-tongues (see also 'Sound-pictures', No. 29.) Get them to make a list of them, in English and other languages.

22 This is only the second poem in the book which *rhymes* throughout (which shows how *in*essential rhyme is to poetry).

Rhyme is one of many ways of giving *shape* to a poem. It is a kind of repetition—we have seen other kinds of repetition in earlier poems. It is very common in English poetry, but it may be pointed out that the Greek, Latin, and older French and English poets did without it, as well as many modern poets.

Rhyme is often difficult for people who are beginning to write. Good rhyme is enjoyable partly because it is like a difficult trick successfully performed: the rhyming word should also be the best word for the *sense* of the line. It is much better to have no rhyme at all than a bad rhyme, which occurs when an unsuitable word is chosen for its rhyme alone.

Rhyme works well in this little poem because it seems quite natural—as if the poet might have used the very same words even if they did not rhyme.

Ask pupils to write a very short rhyming poem. At other times, they can of course use rhymes if they wish, but they should not be told that rhyme is essential.

23 The class should be made to realise the difference in *feeling* between this and the previous poem. No. 22 is light-hearted, whereas this poem is serious, and makes the spider into a kind of monster. Ask the class to find the words which give a feeling of something serious and 'monstrous' going on.

The simple answer to the question about line 4 is that a spider has eight legs; but it also describes the spider's movement, as if crippled.

Ask the class to describe their own feelings about spiders, either orally or in writing.

24 Interest in love-poems depends very much upon the age of the reader. Older pupils might be asked to discuss how well the poem describes the feelings of a boy for a girl, but other aspects can also be discussed. Describing the features of a particular individual is one of the most difficult skills in writing. Discuss whether the poem gives a very clear, individual picture of Lapobo, so that one might recognise her if one met her, or if it is only a general picture.

Get pupils to write a *portrait* of another member of the class or the school—not using their name—so that a reader can recognise who is described. Discuss the *portraits* in class, deciding which gives the clearest picture.

25 This poem has a fine, skipping rhythm and rhyme. It must be read in a lively way to bring out the atmosphere of the story. The poem should first be read by the teacher to illustrate the rhythm. Pupils can then take verses in turn, with the whole class reading the three chorus lines at the end of each verse. Different readers should be given the parts of Mister Bear's friends (verse 3) and Doc Hare himself (verses 3 and 5).

It may take one or two readings before pupils are able to read it fluently.

The last verse may need some explaining. Doc Hare is saying that he will still make money out of his patients, no matter whether they live or die. He is not paid for making people better, but for his knowledge of medicine. Of course, this is nonsense, the opposite of what a doctor should say, and shows what a rogue Doc Hare is. Get the pupils to work out this meaning for themselves, with a little help.

Ask the class to compare this poem with the other Hare poem, No. 18. They are, of course, quite different. Doc Hare behaves like a human being, and the poem tells us more about human beings than animals. But in some ways he is like a hare. Ask them to point out in what ways Doc Hare is like the hare described in the earlier poem.

Get the class to find words whose sound echoes their sense (e.g. 'blam', 'growled', 'howled' etc).

This poem gives ideal material for working up into a play.

26   The poem should be divided between a soloist and chorus, the soloist taking the 1st, 3rd, 5th etc. lines. To emphasise the rocking rhythm, clap with the readers (and get them to clap) on the stressed syllables:

*Nev*er shall I *love* with *one* who is a *bab*y,
(*Joy,* joy, *moth*er, (pause) *this* one sleeps in *inn*ocence)
*Nev*er shall I *love* with *one* who is no *lov*er,
(*Joy,* joy, etc . . .)
I shall love with *one* who is *strong* and brave
                                        and *hand*some,
I shall love with *him* who ap*pears* and causes
                                        *heart*aches,
Yes, I will *have* a *whirl*wind of a *man.*

The speaker(s) can almost shout the word 'whirlwind' in the second-to-last line. This will bring the poem to an effective climax.

27 This poem should not be taken too seriously. The speaker exaggerates to express what he *feels*. He does not really believe that these terrible things will happen to the poor girl.

Discuss the way in which we use exaggeration to express our feelings. For example: 'I was bursting with pride', 'I am jumping for joy', 'I am boiling with anger'. Get pupils to think of other examples or (better) make them up. It will help if you tell them to start with the words: 'I felt like . . .'

28 Get pupils to suggest ways in which a wicked step-mother can be like a crocodile.

Make them write an explanation of exactly what the poem means, as briefly as possible. They will find that they have to use many more words than are in the poem.

The last line is an exclamation, and does not mean anything beyond expressing the speaker's feelings. Ask pupils to make up words which suggest feelings of pleasure, of anger, of surprise.

29 These 'Sound-pictures' give excellent practice in understanding the part sound plays in poetry. At least one class can usefully be spent in learning to speak the sounds so that they convey their meaning to a listener, and in getting pupils to invent their own sound-pictures.

Of course, we use sound-pictures very often in every-day language, in words like 'splash', 'bang' and 'pop'. But it is not a question of finding an already-existing 'correct' word. For instance, pupils may well invent a better word for the crowing of a cock than the usual 'Cock-a-doodle-doo!' The best test is to ask the rest of the class to decide which words sound closest to reality.

30 In the old days before writing song, dance and

poetry were all part of the same activity. This is true in popular songs and dances even today. This poem can be performed so that dance, song and poetry are brought together again. A Ghanaian girl may know how to dance the *Adowa* dance, while others in the class recite the poem. Elsewhere, a suitable local dance should be substituted. Pupils might even make up a tune to suit the words.

They should notice how the poem has the movement of a dance, with variations and repetitions. This can be seen even in the shape of the lines on the page.

A suitable subject for a picture.

31 A rather more difficult poem, though after going through it carefully line-by-line everyone should understand it quite easily. It is difficult because almost every line contains a metaphor. The best way of helping understanding is to ask first, in each line, what does it *seem* to be saying? Then, what is it *really* saying? Thus, the first line *seems* to be saying that the breeze is the rain's father: what it really *means* is that the breeze comes first, and is followed by the rain—as a father is followed by his son. The lines are almost like riddles, and the class should enjoy solving them.

The three short lines in the middle are also metaphors, describing the sound of the thunder as if it were the noise of various animals.

The class can play a variation of the game described in Teacher's Note 7, in which one pupil thinks of an object and describes it by using the form: 'It is like so-and-so', until the others guess the object.

32 This should be read with great liveliness and excitement. Each verse should be given to a different pupil, and each should make his or her verse more dramatic than the previous one. The rest of the class might make the noises of wind, running feet, lightning, thunder

81

and rain in the appropriate places.

Get them to describe, in poetry or prose, the floods which follow the storm.

A very suitable subject for a picture.

33   This lends itself well to dramatization. One pupil can act Agyei, others his attendants and people receiving him and singing his praises. The whole should take the form of a triumphal procession. Ask them to explain why the simile 'like sandals' in the second verse is appropriate, and to explain the 'green mamba' metaphor.

The line 'Agyei the warrior is drunk' is probably also metaphorical, meaning that he has 'red eyes', i.e. is fierce.

Discuss the use of repetition. Repetition can be emphatic, but it can also be boring. Discuss with the pupils which they think it is here.

34   These are the words to a popular American song. If the class sing the song to a suitable tune that is familiar to them, they will be able to pick up the rhythm of the words much more easily.

Let them sing it once or twice first, then speak it while keeping the same rhythm.

Discuss repetition in this poem (compare with No. 29). Ask them how the last verse, which has the same form as the first two, differs in feeling.

Ask what kind of person is speaking the words, what kind of life he leads, etc.

35   The class should be asked to discuss whether they think the poem is rude. Why do foreigners often seem peculiar, or funny, or dangerous? Do pupils think this is right?

Ask them to write a description of themselves as they imagine a stranger might see them. This is a good way of showing how everyone in the world is a foreigner to someone!

36　This poem brings up many important questions about poverty and riches. Why are some people beggars? Is it right to beg? What is it like to be a beggar? How did this man become a beggar? What does he think about as he sits on the pavement? How is it possible to help beggars, besides putting money in the bowl?

Does the writer seem to be sorry for the beggar? Does he suggest that we are right to 'stalk past'? (line 29) The last suggestion in the Pupils' Note can be used as the basis of a small play.

A good subject for a picture.

37　Another poem which was written to be sung. Follow the same method as with No. 34, or use the original tune if this is known. Both this poem and 'Lucky old sun' express thoughts about an after-life. Do the speakers in both poems feel the same about dying? Which attitude does the class agree with, or do they disagree with both?

38　A dramatic comic-horror poem, to be read so as to make the listeners' flesh creep!

The rhythm can be exaggerated without spoiling the poem:

'O *child*ren, *run*, the *Cun*jah *Man*,

Him *mouth* as *big* as *fry*ing *pan*,' etc.

The class will notice that the poem is written in 'bad English'. They should be told that the author knew how to write perfectly good English, but the person who is supposed to be speaking is uneducated. Make them decide what kind of person the speaker is, and what kind of person they think the writer was.

Ask them which parts of the poem they find most exciting, and why.

Ask them to write a story of ghosts or witches, told by an illiterate man.

83

39   Special attention should be paid to the refrain: 'He's Long John,' etc. The 'o' sounds should be as plaintive as possible, and the last four lines should die out to a whisper. Take up the last suggestion in the Pupils' Note by getting the class to write stories about Long John, reading the different versions aloud and comparing them.

40   The main point of the poem lies in the last verse, which should be studied carefully, making sure that everyone knows exactly what it means.
The fourth verse may present some problems. It implies an extra line: '—and he will accept'.
The poem brings up similar questions to those suggested in note 36. Perhaps the most important of all is: 'Is it right that some people are rich and others poor?' Other questions are: Are poor people usually better than rich people, or vice-versa? Are poor people more friendly to each other than rich people? (See the final verse).

41   One reader should take the part of the child and another that of the bird.
Discuss carefully what the last lines mean (see Pupils' Note 1).
Discuss how the rhymes, and the mixture of long and short lines, give the poem a neat shape and clear movement.
Ask the class to suggest other questions, like the child's, which cannot be answered.
A good subject for illustration.

42   Another poem about mystery. Get the class to find images from the poem which are 'half-and-half': the moon shining like the sun; the junction; the ghost himself (half human, half non-human). Most of the lines express a feeling of 'on the one hand this and on the other hand that'.

One reader should be the narrator and the other the ghost.

43 This is a 'dramatic monologue': that is, a dramatic poem with only one 'actor'—except for the 'Madam's' two lines in the second-to-last verse, which should be read by someone else.

Several topics for discussion are suggested in the Pupils' Notes. Another important one is: 'Does the 'Madam' really love Alberta as she says she does?

The poet was American. Pupils may feel that a similar situation in their country would happen rather differently. Encourage them to imagine what *would* happen, using · the appropriate language for the 'Madam' and her servant.

44 These riddles are good examples of the way in which metaphors work, and making up riddles is an excellent way for pupils to practise using language metaphorically.

Some time should be spent working out how the riddles fit their meanings, until the class has fully grasped the idea.

They may well know some riddles already. Collect as many examples as possible and discuss in each case how the solution fits the riddle. Note that a great many riddles take the form: of 'Why is a __ like a __?'—in other words, they are similes.

45 A large proportion of literature throughout the world is, like this poem, comic. Ask the class why this should be. Why do people like reading nonsense? Why do people make the extraordinary noise called *laughter*? What things make them laugh? And why? Ask the class to give examples of things they find funny, and—more difficult—try to explain why they laugh at them.

46   This poem is a little difficult because the poet suggests more than he actually says. When the poem has been read, pupils can see that the title suggests something like: 'This is supposed to be 'western civilization', but really it is much worse than the old way of life.' This irony is echoed throughout the poem. Help the pupils to recognise this with regard to Pupils' Notes 1, 2 and 4.

Discuss how the repetition of lines 10—17 adds to the sense of the words.

Discuss whether the poet is right to describe western civilization in this way.

47   Pupils' Note 3 will give plenty of opportunity for discussion: it is another question which has never been fully answered.

It is sometimes said that poems should be about beautiful things. Many of the poems in this and other anthologies are about things which certainly are not beautiful (the previous poem, for example). Discuss why this should be so.

48   One of the harder poems in the book, which needs careful study. The class should work out together, exactly what the poem tells them about the writer's family, and what happened to the coconuts. After they have understood the plain sense of the poem, ask them if it reminds them of their own childhood. Ask them what they remember most clearly from their childhood, and why; also, what 'growing-up' means, how it is described in the poem, and whether they think young children have different feelings from those of older children or adults.

49   Pupils may well ask whether they are expected to take this creation story as the truth. It should be pointed out to them that even if the creation did not actually happen in this way, it may tell us a lot about

the way in which human beings think about the big
questions of life and death.

Each section should be given to a different narrator,
with other voices reading the parts of Kizumu and God.
The whole poem can be turned into a play with parts
for God, Sun, Moon, Rain, Darkness, Kiyomba,
Kizumu, the Younger Wife, Death, Life and Soul.
Extra dialogue should be made up, for the quarrel
between Kiyomba and his wife (line 19), the choosing
of the baskets (lines 24—32), the journey (lines 36—
42), and so on.

50 Use this poem as the basis for a discussion about the
    differences between people's attitudes towards each
    other. Compare it with No. 35.